AF241812

When the Wild Things Mend

On Hurt, Healing, and Heritage

Sahar A. Dandan

Daybreak Press
3533 Lexington Avenue North, Arden Hills, MN 55126
www.rabata.org/daybreakpress | daybreakpress@rabata.org

ISBN (print): 978-1-967369-08-9
ISBN (ebook): 978-1-967369-09-6
LCCN: 2025946270

Cover design and typesetting: Studio Zena | www.studiozena.com.au
Printed in the United States of America

Dedication

*In the name of God, the Most Gracious,
the Most Merciful.*

To the keepers of my words.

To my sisters of ink and understanding, who read my
verses, collected my scattered whispers and bound
them with a ribbon and gifted them to me. You carried
these pages to doorways I would never think to knock
on—your hands, thoughts, and responses were the first
publishing house that mattered.

To the women who wept in the margins, your tears
anointed these lines, and in their salt tracks, may the
tin women rust enough to find their heartbeats.

To my mother—your silence taught me the grammar
of resilience. To her mother—your prayers hum in my
hyphenated blood. To the matriarchs before them who
planted orchards in their scars so we might taste the
sweetness of their fruit.

To my father—whose love was a language of rough
hands and raised bars, and whose silence taught me to
listen for the words inside the wound. I keep his steel in
my voice, his hunger in my bones, and the horizons he
taught me to chase in my sights.

To my husband, my sanctuary, in whose embrace I
hear his mother's echoes. I see her in your thoughtful
gestures, your unwavering spirit, and the joy you nurture
in our children. Her belief in their limitless potential now
flows through your hands, your words, your love, as we
raise them with the fire she gifted us.

To my daughters and son, may you inherit not just
our fire but the right to burn unapologetically. To your
daughters unborn, may you read these words one day
and know that your voice was dreamed into existence
long before your first breath.

To my sisters, you're the only ones who knew the weight
of silence before we spoke. To my brothers, who became
safe harbors without being asked. We were never just
siblings. We were the first country we ever belonged to.
To the wives of my brothers, who love the men we once
knew as boys and spin from that love a new language
their children speak fluently.

To my nieces and nephews, daughters and sons of my
heart, bridges between blood and chosen kin. May
you carry your mothers' courage like lamps through
shadowed paths. May your rebellions bloom gardens
where our thorns once grew, and may your submission
be only to God.

To my sisters by blood and battle, who wear their
cracks like gold kintsugi. To the aunties who became
lighthouses, the cousins who became compasses,
the chosen family who said "Here, I'll be your witness."

This is not a book I wanted to write
This felt like a communal meal
I needed to cook without following a recipe
but from the knowing
of generations of grit and grace
cooked in the fire of collective grief
served warm to every woman
who's ever had to stitch her mouth shut
only to reopen it in song

Carry it forward
Pass it sideways
Shelter it in your chests
We survive in circles
not lines
With a heart wider than any wound can make

Contents

Foreword

. . . . *page 1*

Prologue

. . . . *page 4*

01. Acknowledgment

. . . . *page 8*

02. Mother as a First Language

. . . . *page 11*

03. Tayta

. . . .*page 13*

04. Vowels of Survival

. . . . *page 16*

05. The Alphabet of Survival

. . . . *page 20*

06. When the Wild Things Mend

. . . . *page 23*

07. Rooms That Remember

. . . . *page 25*

08. Kintsugi for the Living

. . . . *page 27*

09. Obituary for the Unremembered

. . . . *page 29*

10. Broken Story حكاية مكسورة

. . . . *page 31*

11. My Dearest Daughter

. . . . *page 34*

12. Inventory of Absence

. . . . *page 44*

13. What the River Refuses to Carry

. . . . *page 46*

14. Her Hands Could Not Unlearn

. . . . *page 48*

15. The Art of Shrinking

. . . . *page 54*

16. Origami Whispers

. . . . *page 56*

17. Through Her Pleasure, His Mercy

. . . . *page 58*

18. To the Mother I Remember

. . . . *page 61*

19. Here and There

. . . . *page 65*

20. What We Carry ما نحمله

. . . . *page 68*

21. The Essence of Us

. . . . *page 72*

22. The Space Between

. . . . *page 76*

23. Inheritance

. . . . *page 78*

24. Safety Once Had a Scent

. . . . *page 82*

25. Beacons of Light

. . . . *page 86*

Afterword

. . . . *page 93*

About the Author

. . . . *page 95*

Foreword

The room was dimly lit, the audience alive with anticipation. Sahar Dandan stood before us—not merely to lecture, but to unveil a road of learning paved with hardship, devotion, and grace. She spoke of her time in Mauritania: sun-scorched desert days and bone-chilling nights, caves, tents, and long treks for her most basic human needs. She spoke of grief, of isolation, of the uphill struggle to be granted permission to learn from the revered teachers of that land. And then—her joy. The turning point. The moment the gates of sacred knowledge opened to her.

Sahar would go on to become the only foreign woman to study directly with the great Shaykh Murabit al-Hajj, whose knowledge ran as deep and wide as the ocean, whose name was synonymous with virtue and piety and whose life was an example of devotion and commitment. That she was chosen for this path was no accident. It was, without doubt, a Divine selection.

To meet Sahar is to encounter a woman of rare intensity, guided by sincerity, clarity of purpose, and an unwavering concern for the ummah. She is brilliant—yes—but not in the distant, unreachable way we sometimes imagine brilliance. Hers is a grounded, luminous intellect, paired with real warmth and generosity. (She also happens to be one of the best cooks I've ever met. On the day I was

invited into her home, she served an Italian meal
with bread and gnocchi made from scratch!)

In this book, you are invited into her world. You are
given the rare opportunity to sit at the feet of a scholar,
to drink from the flowing river of her knowledge, wisdom,
and cultural insight.

This is not simply a book of poems. It is an honest
companion for anyone in search of meaning. The words
here will meet you where you are, press on your emotions,
and reshape you from the inside out.

Sahar Dandan revives an ancient and sacred craft:
that of the scholar-poet. In her hands, poetry becomes
not only art, but a vessel of transmission—of truth,
of tradition, of love. She shows us that when knowledge
is wrapped in beauty, it reaches us more deeply and
stays longer.

May we be among those who truly listen.

Dr. Tamara Gray
Arden Hills, Minnesota, September 2025

The womb is
a room with
many doors.

Prologue

This is not a book about mothers and daughters.

This is a book about language—
the kind we inherit in the spaces between
a woman's silence and her scream.
There is no language for inheritance that
does not taste of both honey and salt.
The vocabulary passed down like a birthright:
how to say no with your spine
When your lips won't move,
How to stitch a warning into the hem of a lullaby.

This is not a book about loss.
This is a book about excavation—
About the hands that sift through the rubble
of what was never said
To find the bones of a story still humming.

My mother's voice was a country I crossed
without a map.
Her silence a dialect I learned to speak fluently.
Her mother's silence a scripture written in the
margins of old letters.
We do not mourn what we never held, but we
bend before its ghost.

Here is what never made it into their lessons:
The weight of a word swallowed too many times.
The way silence grows teeth if you feed it enough fear.

I have spent my life translating the space between
what was said and what was meant.

Between the hand that strikes
and the hand that soothes
When both belong to the same body.

This is not a book of answers.
It is a map of the wounds that taught us how to walk.
A record of how we learned to make ink from our own
blood when the world refused us pens.

Like the nectaries, those tiny glands at the base of a
flower that weep sugar
Long after the bloom has fallen,
This is how we love our mothers:
In the aftermath.
In the unasked questions.
In the way we mimic their gestures without meaning to,
Our hands shaping the air the way theirs once did over
a stove
A wound
A child's fevered forehead.

This book is a house with all the doors left open.
Step inside.
The air here smells of turned earth and
unfinished business.
Somewhere ahead, a daughter is spelling her name

When the Wild Things Mend

for the first time—
her mouth shaping the letters her mother never
got to speak.
A mother teaching herself to read the braille of old scars.
A grandmother's laugh trapped in a jar of apricot jam.

Here, survival is a verb with no past tense.

Begin here,
where the light slips
in through the cracks.

01

Acknowledgment

I acknowledge and honor the mothers
whose bodies became our first universe
wombs stitching stardust into spine
blood into breath

To the grandmothers who wove survival
into our sinew
their hands mapping alphabets
only the broken can read

I honor the daughters
who inherited not just broken stories
but the molten gold to mend them

To the Taytas whose tongues
held dialects of toughness
who spun hope from hunger
laughter from loss
your silenced anthems
hum in our marrow

I acknowledge the women
who planted orchards in war-torn soil
whose prayers became our compass

To survivor mothers
to mothers whose children were murdered

to mothers whose light was dimmed
your lullabies louder than bombs
your shattered hearts are our boils that never healed

I carry the ones who walked barren
but birthed revolutions
who turned their scars into scripture

This book is a needle threaded with your light
darning the gaps between her and history

For the daughters not yet born
may these poems be a womb

*Some memories arrive
without permission.*

02

Mother as a First Language

She breathed words into
The mess of letters

She weaved dreams
Out of the mismatch
The jumbled up
Mixed-up
Make-no-sense
Alphabet soup

She put in order
My chaos

I owe her my words
Knitted into dreams
Woven into stories
Making sense
Of the nonsensical

Making my imagination
  Soar

Making me
  Believe in myself

Faith reawakened
In the beauty of me

When the Wild Things Mend

Only now I have no words
To show her my love
My inability
To let her know

That she brightened my world
With her colors
That she watered my seedling
When I was in drought

That she instilled hope
When others gave up

Her
Heaven under her feet
Mum

03

Tayta

I sit at your feet
A spindle of girlhood
Spun from your voice
Pondering your face
As you weave stories
As you knit your woolen cardigan

Each know a warning
Each stitch a spell
As you murmur "Winter is coming"
"Snow may surround us" you say
"But our blood is hot"
And you gaze upon my face
And smile
"Yours is fire"

You march us through forests
Where shadows chase our ankles
And light pools like spilled honey
You taught us the names of monsters
We sailed through oceans of storms
Fighting serpents and faceless creatures
Bravery was a given

And now the monsters I can't get rid of
Silence
Expectation

When the Wild Things Mend

Tayta
A mother to my mother
A grandmother to us
But grand does not begin to describe your grandeur
Grand only in the way mountains
Are called hills on maps
Drawn by small hands
Unable to give them their true stature

Grand cannot bring together
The image of your lips moving
To tell us stories of past heroines
Of women too smart for their own good
Who hid their sharpness
Inside soft fairy tales

I learned to hide
To be small in their spaces
I learned to fold
To fit myself inside the hollows
Of expectation
I learned to be silent
Even as my blood's fire screamed
I swallowed my hunger
that begged for a tongue
And I let the flames
burn me

Tayta
Your unstoppable fingers
  Braiding my hair
Tucking rebellion into every strand
Your cheeky smile
  As you put fear in our hearts
Of fallen heroines
And the chaos of rebellion
I feared your stories
Until I became one
A girl who split her tongue
On the word no
Who learned to stitch her name
With her own blood and tears

Grand? No
You are the loom
The wool
The blistered hands
Still weaving
Grand is such a little word for a persona so enthralling
Long after your worldly light fades

04

Vowels of Survival

Every daughter learns the alphabet of betrayal
before she learns to spell her own name
our mothers teach us
the vowels of survival

This is the inheritance no one talks about
at the cradle
the way trust breaks like a language
whose vowels bleed into consonants of caution

A lineage of women before me
learned to map deceit in braille
fingers reading the raised scars
left by "kind" hands that shattered trust
and called the debris sacrifice

We were raised on paradoxes
while their knives gleamed
know they are not your friends
when they borrow your light
just to shadow your path
when they break your bones
and call the fragments your fault

No one warned us about the consonants
the hard edges of treachery that lodge in the throat
passed down as inheritance

like cherry pits
wondering if we should swallow them
or spit them out

The mothers before me forgot to include
instructions for the poison
so I'll write them now
for the daughters after
like the shorthand notes
our mothers scrawled in the margins
in invisible ink
blooming visible under our rage

They will try to shrink your ocean
to the size of their puddle
let them choke on the salt
let them whine in their shallow ponds
you are a daughter of riptides
every word they twisted into weaponry
becomes another letter
you steal back
for our survival script

Hold my hand and feel it
that old, familiar fracture
when I first tasted venom
in their sugared words

just as I did when their smile
oozed honey over daggered teeth

Take comfort in the ink of our lineage
my daughter
feel how my "No" now forms
quicker than my "Maybe" ever did
trace the braille of these invisible lessons
with fingers already wiser than mine

They tried to teach me
better the enemy you know than the wolf
who may lurk on the road you've never walked
I was not made to stay where harm
felt familiar

I unlearned their logic
chose paths without signs
where silence taught me to listen
and wrong turns led me back to myself

I had to learn the alphabet anew
to steal my letters back
to wrap vowels around their consonants
so my words could make sense
words I once bled for
now wielded like a blade

I take comfort in the henna of our integrity
how it stains deeper than their ephemeral paint
know that the storm in our veins cannot be measured
by the thimblefuls they call truth

The mothers before us left spaces
between their warnings
room enough for our pens
to bloom gardens where their thorns once grew

And you
you will rewrite this alphabet
with ink mixed from their swallowed pits
and the iron forged in the fire
of our welded tongues

05

The Alphabet of Survival

We are the ashes
  of every blaze we set alight
Burn marks on feet not afraid
  treading on embers
Smudges on singed fingers
  still breathing fire

We are the letters
  scrawled like lifelines
  in the margins of each other's stories
  unreadable sometimes
  fading but never erased

You were my first language
Your hands spelling out survival
  in lullabies sharpened with warnings
  in whispers that carried storms

The fire of myself
  is not a friend
  it sears, blisters, scars
  leaves me coughing
  on my own smoke

We love imperfectly
Because we are the ache

of words left unsaid
of boundaries drawn in fear, not hate

But whole still
Like roots tangled beneath the earth
knotted with secrets and silence
nourishing the same tree

We are the mirror
that fractures
Each shard reflecting you whole
Seeing you
in my face
through the cracks

In the curve of my frown
In the echo of your no
In the rhythm of prayers
You taught me with trembling hands
There I find you still

We are the broken alphabet
Still trying to spell out
The survivors
The aching
The breaking
The carrying each other

Even when we are tired
Even when we are far
We write and rewrite
The story of us

In the breath of smoke
In the ink of fire
In the gleam of healing scars

06

When the Wild Things Mend

I remember her hands their porcelain skin
mapped with a thousand fractures
I remember how the cracks would shine
if you turned them toward the sun
I remember she held me tight
while everything around us shattered

Every day
we woke to more broken things
mending with what we had
I thought breaking would scatter us
but she picked up threads I didn't know were there

I watched how the wild things mend
not with clean lines, but with jagged grace
every suture a rebellion
every knot a covenant

She told me we will wear our repairs
like maps to somewhere
better than unbroken
each crack a corridor
each seam a doorway
the light could slip through

Her hands taught me
that a vessel does not fail

because it was broken
it becomes a lantern
its light spilling
through every place
that was once shattered

Mum
here I stand
and no one can tell
where the wildness ends
and the healing begins
my vessel whole and overflowing
no glass half empty
but brimming with the sky
I want you to know
that I owe you
for not staying broken forever
for knowing even the wild things can mend

07

Rooms That Remember

A garden
An oasis
A mind filled with ideas
A heart full of love
A home that once held comfort
Shelves lined with books
Drives storing memories
Boxes hiding fragments of us
Notebooks filled with Post-its
Rooms scattered with toys
Walls heavy with photos
Corners cradling mementos

A kitchen
Once warm with laughter
And late-night tears
A couch
Worn from long talks
And longer silences
Drawers spilling
Things we forgot we needed
A hallway
That no longer echoes your steps

A scent
I can't name
But know as yours

When the Wild Things Mend

A shadow
The sun keeps trying to cast
A silence
Louder than any sound
A space
Nothing fills

The house does not forget
Its walls breathe your name
Every room
Remembers you
In its own language

08

Kintsugi for the Living

Each of us
A mosaic of joy and sadness
Laughter salt-dried by tears

We kneel in the wreckage
Palms upturned
Sorting shards
Here
  your grandmother's silence
There
  my cracked defiance

We glue them with gold
Not to hide the breaks
But to make the seams glow

Look how we hold it now
This fragile
  lopsided vessel

Leaking light from every scar
A thing of terrible beauty
Broken and refired
Rebuilt with jagged lines of gold
Still
  We hold
Still
  We pour

When the Wild Things Mend

For the daughters
Who will drink life
From our priceless cracks

09

Obituary for the Unremembered

A woman barely has to die
Before she is folded into silence
Her name erased like a chalkboard theorem
Her work stitched into a man's coat
As if her hands were never calloused
    From the weaving

Worth is a matter of opinion
Opinion is a child of culture
And our culture? A boy king
Sucking the marrow from his mother's bones
    Then praising his own hunger

But listen
We are the daughters
Who dig up the unmarked graves
We scream into the abyss between us
To shatter the silence
Until it coughs up your theorems
Your sonnets
    your cures for forgetting

We glue your legacy back together
With spit and gold leaf
And when they ask whose hands did this?

We will say
Hers
And ours
And the daughters after

10

Broken Story حكاية مكسورة

(When I told you the story)   لما حكيتلك الحكاية
It was a fable of the daughter
I thought I'd birth
Golden, obedient
A mirror polished smooth enough
To reflect my own mother's hands

(It was our story, a love story)   كانت قصتنا قصة حب
But love is a knife that carves
Before it feeds. I sharpened it
On my dreams for you

(And when I told our story)   ولما أنا حكيت حكايتنا
I buried your rebellions
Under folktales
How you split my seams
With your tempest marrow
How your laughter scorched
The delusions of my expectations

(I forgot your story)   نسيت حكايتك
Until I saw you stitch your name
Into the spine of a book
They said a woman shouldn't write

When the Wild Things Mend

(Every memory)   كل ذكرة
Is a funeral for the girl I imagined
And a birth cry for the woman
Who outgrew my lullabies

For what we lost...

and found.

11

My Dearest Daughter

How and where do I begin?
All I can do
is guide
and pray for guidance

A is for Acceptance, the brave first step of seeing
your reflection in the fractured glass of false mirrors
where society's shadows distort your true shape
recognizing that even shattered pieces carry beauty

B is for Brokenness, which we have both known
not as a curse, but as a doorway
through which the light of understanding seeps in
wrapping us softly in its quiet grace

C is for Connection, the thread that ties us
to the memories of past sorrows
and to the hope of future mornings
exposing our vulnerabilities
each tear and every sigh a hidden verse

D is for Determination, born from those moments
when the world presses down and you learn
that strength is sometimes found
in the delicate act of surrendering
of allowing yourself to be reshaped
by an alchemist

with a fire that burns you
tempers and molds you
with love that is both fierce and tender

E is for Empathy, a gift only the wounded can offer
a wisdom that blossoms among the ruins
transforming our deepest pain into a soft, enduring
strength
I hope you learn, as I did, that to be broken
is not to be defeated, but to be reborn
into a light that shines all the more brilliantly
against the shadows of life's imperfection

My daughter, my heart

I write to you with a heart that remembers
all the nights we cried in the silence of our solitude
and all the mornings we rose
fragile yet defiant
embracing the art of survival

Know that every trial is a letter in our story
each one contributing
to the song of our resilience

F is for Faith, a steady flame that glimmers
even in the darkest hours

to remind you that you are never truly alone
even when the night seems endless
let your faith be the soft murmur of a lullaby
that eases your fears and cradles your spirit

(F is also always and forever for Forgiveness,
the quiet revolution
that begins not in grand gestures
but in the reluctant decision to release
what your heart was never meant to carry
it is the river that finds a path between boulders
the wind that lifts the ash of old wounds
and scatters them into forgetting
forgiveness not to excuse the harm
but to free you from its leash
a defiant act of mercy
offer it first to yourself
then to the past
then to the world)

G is for Grace, the gentle art of accepting who you are
with all your jagged edges
and the wild geography of your wounds
remember, my love
grace is not found in flawless perfection
but in the way you rise after each fall
each stumble writing a new verse

H is for Healing, a slow, rhythmic dance between
sorrow and hope
where each sharp and flat
tune your melody of recovery
in those moments of solitude
allow the act of healing to be your rebellion
a testament to your profound strength
built on the multitude of women who survived
before you
and after you

I is for Insight, gleaned from those midnight
conversations with your own soul
when you ponder the mysteries of your existence
when the brutality of our honesty
tears us apart
and you realize that your scars
are maps to the hidden treasure of your wisdom
may you always seek the lessons
within each trial
knowing they don't diminish you

J is for Journey, the uncharted path
that you walk with hesitance and unyielding resolve
know that each step
even the uncertain ones
brings you closer

to the person you are meant to become
the journey is not measured by miles
but by the courage in every heartbeat
and the whispers of your undying will

K is for Kindness, to yourself and others
let kindness be the ink that writes your story
infusing every line with compassion and understanding
even if you feel beaten and trodden upon
in a world that often celebrates perfection
choose to honor the beauty of your imperfections
for they are the mirror of a true life lived

My Daughter, my love

As you continue to gather the letters of this alphabet
a collection of survival, of resurgence, of rebirth
know that each letter is a beacon
lighting the way through the maze of life
and remember that every fragment of your being
is a stanza
in the poem of our shared legacy

L is for Love, an all-encompassing embrace that flows
without limits
that nurtures our wounds and fills our emptiness
with a warmth only the heart can understand

may you discover love in the quiet hum of life
and in the deepest corners of your spirit

M is for Mercy, a reprieve granted in moments of our
weakness
an assurance that even in our failings
we are wrapped in compassion
remember, my child, that mercy is both a gift
and a reminder of the infinite grace that sustains us

N is for Newness, a constant promise
that each dawn invites us to begin again
to see our scars not as end points but as portals
to stronger, brighter versions of ourselves
let each morning whisper of new possibilities
and every sunset nurture many tomorrows

O is for Opportunity, the chance to reframe our story
to write on blank pages with bold strokes
of courage and creativity, even when the ink is
made with our own tears
in every setback, find the seeds of a comeback
knowing life offers constant chances to bloom anew

P is for Persistence, the rhythm of your resilient heart
that beats even through the fiercest storms
this determination, though quiet and humble

is your anchor in turbulent times, a reminder
that you are built to weather the toughest of gales

Q is for Quiet, those silent interludes
where reflection ponders on the greatness of the Divine
in these pauses, listen closely to your inner voice
for it is here that the humility of your soul
reveals itself in sincere gratitude

R is for Resilience, a tapestry woven
from threads of hope, even in moments of despair
may you rise, again and again, from the fragments of
yesterday
discovering that your strength grows
with every challenge embraced

S is for Surrender, a tender release that transforms
struggle into strength
let go of the need to control the outcome
trust instead in the Divine plan that guides you
finding freedom in the vulnerability of your truth
and in true submission to the Divine will

T is for Transformation, a sacred journey
from the raw pain of brokenness to the serene
beauty of rebirth
each piece of your splintered self is reassembled

by the quiet hand of time, sculpting you into
a radiant testament to life's endless capacity to heal

U is for Understanding, the soft insight that blossoms
when we confront our deepest wounds with honesty
may you always seek to understand yourself
and in doing so, discover the boundless empathy
that connects all our hearts across time and space

V is for Valor, a quiet bravery that dares to be seen
even when fear casts long shadows upon your path
your strength lies not in the absence of faltering
but in every step taken despite the uncertainties ahead

W is for Wisdom, a gentle, chaotic culmination
of every lesson learned along this winding journey
let your wisdom be the light that guides your way
a lantern crafted from both joy and sorrow
to illuminate even the darkest of paths

X is for the unknown, a mystery we all must explore
the spaces between the known letters
where imagination and destiny intertwine
embrace this uncertainty
for it is the canvas upon which your life is painted

Y is for Yes, the quiet affirmation to life
despite the echoes of doubt and fear

say yes to each moment, each chance for growth
and watch as your world transforms
with every brave, gentle yes you offer the horizon

Z is for Zenith, a peak that represents not an end
but a continuous cycle of rising, shining
and returning to the earth to begin again
let your zenith be a reminder that you are ever in motion
ever evolving
ever a brilliant verse in this poem of survival

My Dearest Daughter,

May this alphabet of survival be your companion
a cherished map crafted with the ink of our shared
sorrows
and the light of our profound triumphs
a secret of divine mercy waiting to be whispered
into the ear of your brave, resilient soul

Our journey, written in the language of loss
and composed in the free verse of our heartbeats
teaches us life is not endurance
but the art of rising again and again
into a love that nurtures every frail
hopeful part of you

Carry these letters close to your heart
and let them be the gentle words that guide you
through every chapter of your magnificent journey

With all the love in my heart,
Your ever-admiring mother

With all the hope my hands can hold,
Your ever-admiring mother

With endless love and unwavering faith in you,
Your ever-admiring mother

12

Inventory of Absence

A garden grows wild with silence
each petal a breath you didn't take
a symphony of clocks all ticking
toward the hour you might still arrive

Here the mind is an attic
dusty shelves bowing under the weight
of unread books, their spines cracked
with questions you left unanswered

The heart a drawer jammed with letters
ink smudged by thumbs hoping to
erase the dates
walls papered in photos
your face a ghost in every frame

Flash drives hum with vacations
we didn't take with you
pixels frozen mid-laugh
boxes cough up ticket stubs
dried roses
a gold chain missing its pendant

Even the filing cabinets churn
folders fat with grocery lists
things to do
your handwriting a relic

the closet in the corner still whispers
hide-and-seek
though no one counts to ten

Every corner a museum
every room a throat
choked on the almost
   the yet-to-be-done
      the leftovers

And the house
so full of memories
so full of ache
bends and breaks
and reshapes itself
around the empty shape
of you
missing

13

What the River Refuses to Carry

I am the daughter of drought
Raised by a well that always ran dry
The earth here memorizes absences
As the roots of trees grow teeth
And the sky forgets
That it's above

They say grief is a language
That only the unloved translate fluently
I speak it in seasons
Spring, when new growth blooms
Except where I was planted
Summer, when the wind stuffs my mouth
With the ashes of unread letters
Autumn, when loss blushes in golden hues
Beauty in the letting go
Winter, when the muddiness of the earth
Fills every crevice in my body

She sang me a hymn
With a mouth full of blades
Every verse left me bleeding
Every chorus a velvet bruise

I branded the lyrics on my tongue
Breathed the smoke into my skull
Where it sings itself silently

On Hurt, Healing, and Heritage

Soundtrack to my words
A lullaby for the unwanted

I asked the river to carry her shadow
Back to me. She laughed, said:
Water only mourns what it cannot drown
So I became the current
The cold
  The frost
    The flood
The thing that slips through
Every fractured vessel

What couldn't hold me
Wore me down
And when they find my bones
Bleached and wind-scoured
They'll mistake them for ruins
Let them

I've learned
To build my worth
From what the light abandoned

14

Her Hands Could Not Unlearn

My mother's voice was a threadbare quilt
She mended my silence with stories
Of women who planted orchards in their wrists
Roots climbing their throats

   Fruit blooming
From every no
     they were never allowed to speak
From every yes
     they were forced to utter

I learned to sew my buttons by watching her
Thread the needle by candlelight
Picking greenery from cliff faces
Turning hunger into something sacred
This is how you survive
    she'd say
Steal sweetness from the sting

Her palms mapped with roads she never walked
Each crease a rebellion smuggled
Beneath her dry, callused skin
At night
    she'd comb my hair
Trying to straighten its curly insurrection
Let loose a river of grief
I'd mistake for lullabies

On Hurt, Healing, and Heritage

Once
    I found her weeping into dough
Kneading loss into loaves
For a man who never tasted her tears

Daughter
    she warned
Don't love too much
Don't laugh too loud
Joy is a debt
    this world collects in blood

I grew teeth from the sugar she hid
    In my milk
Fists from the spices she ground
    Into my name
Voice from the fairy tales
    She dared not finish
Bones from the loom
    Where she wove our worth
Into rugs meant to hold
A man's unclean feet

I unravel the threads
Knot them into a ladder
Climb toward a dawn

When the Wild Things Mend

She never named me
    But hummed into my cradle
A tune only the scarred
    Can carry

Now I sing with her buried fury
A wildfire rock song
That cracks the walls
Where they begged her
    To burn quiet

Mother
    I am the echo that refuses to fade
I shake the broken tiles
    they made you cover
I am the tremor
    in their foundation
The groan
    beneath their polished floors

Mother
    I wear your hunger
Like a crown
What you buried
    I dig into
With these wolf-teeth
This throat of ember and prayer

You were told
To dissolve like salt in blood
I am the iron
    they could not remove
      they could not bend

You were told
To dissolve like sugar in tea
Your sugar now rots their teeth
Your spices now sting their eyes
And the voice you forged
In the dark?

It becomes the storm
Becomes the thought

They'll learn to fear
In daughters

Mother
Now your mirror claims my face
And I wear your fears like heirlooms
The gold you melted to pay for my wings
The ache you called love
That bends my spine into a question mark

When the Wild Things Mend

When she died, I inherited her ghosts
The girl she buried to become a mother
The wars she swallowed to keep me soft
And now I stitch her silence into my daughter's coat
Tell her this is armor
Tell her this is how we stay alive

There are silences
that say more than
speech ever could.

15

The Art of Shrinking

Mum
You taught us the geometry of survival
How to make ourselves smaller
How to occupy less space
How to dissolve into the wallpaper
Before anyone thought to peel us away

We became experts in the calculus of risk
Measuring every word
Every gesture
Subtracting desire before it could be seen
Dividing ourselves into fractions
Just to keep the whole from breaking

But Mum
Survival is not the same as living
You gave us the gift of endurance
But not the directions to find ourselves
We learned to bend
But not how to stand
We learned to whisper
But not how to roar

And now
When I watch you
Hold your hands together
I wonder if you ever dreamed

Of opening them wide
Not in surrender to the wind
But in supplication

We are done with shrinking
We are learning to take up space
To let our voices crack the plaster
To unlearn the safety of silence

Mum,
I forgive you
    the folded hands
      the swallowed thunder
you fed us survival
on a spoon bent backward

But watch now
as we unfold
    your origami daughters
      unpressing each crease
        into swords
          into wings
        into maps
        of territories
      you were never
allowed to name

16

Origami Whispers

You learned the language of small things
  to fold your voice into origami whispers
    to tuck your thoughts into the corners of rooms
Where no one would trip over them

You learned to be fog
  to arrive without arrival
    to vanish without leaving
      to haunt the edges of yourself
So no one would call it rebellion

You learned to smile
  a curve, not a confession
    to laugh but never too loud
      to soften your edges before anyone
      asked you to
        to carry your storm in a teacup
And make it look graceful

You learned to disappear without leaving the room
  kept your rage like a pressed flower
    between pages no one opened
      to count exits with your eyes
To name silence
  by its temperature
    its taste

its shape as it pressed on your lungs
to steal your breath

You spoke in Morse code
Short bursts of sound
for safe
for silent
for don't
Sentences pared down to the bone
Just enough to feed the hunger
Never enough for them
to choke on

17

Through Her Pleasure, His Mercy

We were told to fear God
But never how His mercy moves
Through my mother's tired sigh
How His justice rests
In the arch of her weary foot

Obey, said the Quran
And they carved it into your spine
Like a pillar for heaven's gate
But did they teach you
How angels pause
To catch a mother's whispered alhamdulillah
Over sleeping children?

I learned prayer by watching
Her hands pour water at fajr
Her forehead's imprint
Deeper than mine would ever be
God's command lives here
Not in the roar of threats
But in the honey of her morning du'a
Still warm in my veins

The scholars argue over which door
To Paradise opens widest
I know it's the one
That smells of her hands' oil

And the salt of her hidden tears
Her displeasure shakes the Throne
More than any sin ever could
For who dares anger the One
Who chose her as His vessel?

We measure our submission to God
By the weight of her slippers
In our upturned palms
Not because we fear Hellfire
But because we've seen
How the light enters our home

When the angels ask
What good deeds I bring
I'll lay down every "Yes, Ummi"
Like rose petals at the gate
Each one a key
Forged in the furnace
Of her silent sacrifices

And when the Scale trembles
With the weight of my deeds
I'll place her contentment
Soft as dates at iftar
Sweet as the ameen after du'a
On the golden plate

When the Wild Things Mend

Knowing this:
Her smile was the mosque
Where I learned to bow
Her lap the Kaaba
That taught me direction

So let my "Yes, Ummis" be bricks
Building the bridge to Janna
Each one laid with the mortar
Of her forgiving sighs

For when Allah asks
"How did you honor My trust?"
I'll point to the dust
Still clinging to my forehead
From prostrating to Him at her door

And praying
Let her pleasure be the compass
That leads me to Your pleasure
And her satisfied heart
The mirror reflecting
Your eternal mercy

18

To the Mother I Remember

Your hands that patched my knees
Now tremble holding pills
Your stories that filled the dark
Are now lost in medication schedules
How cruel... this reversal
Me holding the umbrella now
While your storms rage inward

When the nurses say you don't remember
I taste our old laughter like stolen lollies
When you ask my name
I give it like a love letter
Every blank stare
Becomes a fresh page
Where I rewrite our joy

How I remember
When you entered rooms
And they rearranged themselves
Around your presence
Chairs sat up straighter
Lights burned brighter
Even the air held its breath
Waiting for your verdict

You were no mere woman
But a force contained in skin

When the Wild Things Mend

A hurricane in human form
Who could silence arguments
With one raised eyebrow
Command respect
With the simple folding of your hands

Now the world sits careless
Unaware of the earthquake
That's gone quiet within you
They don't see how the walls
Still lean slightly toward you
How the shadows part
Out of ancient habit

When I walk into rooms now
I try to stand the way you did
Shoulders back like I own the air
Chin up like I know my worth

Because if I can't have you here
At least I can carry
Your unbreakable posture
Your unshakable fire
The way you taught the world
To make space for you

On Hurt, Healing, and Heritage

The wound stays open
Not because you're gone
But because love was never meant
To be sealed tight
It bleeds
It aches
It cries out

And I want this endless missing
To be the proof
You were here
You were mine

And no absence
Can unmother you from me

A daughter's wound is never healed
When the mother I remember
Is not there anymore

I see you
And it hurts to see
Your laughter that rang so loud
Now folded like a fraying prayer rug
Too fragile to unfold
I don't know how to not miss you
I don't know how to not love you

When the Wild Things Mend

I don't know how to move on
I don't know how to stop
Wishing for you in the dark
When fever hits
And your touch is all I crave

But here is what I know
When they say your name
And you stare blankly
I become the remembering
When they say you're gone
I become the archive

You are
   in the way I stand my ground
   in the way I refuse to shrink
   in the way my laughter
   suddenly sounds like yours
   still forcing the world
   to make space

I am the earthquake now
For both of us

19

Here and There

I wish you here
I wish you here

To see
All the joy you left behind
All the moments that
Would have been better
If you were only here

I wish you here
Every day
Every moment I see
The love you built
Still catching the light
In the shape of your name

I wish you here
Every time
Your caring touch is needed
When the dark presses close
And I remember how your voice
Turned fear into a lullaby

Do you think of us
And the laughter we shared
How your arms were the only shelter
That ever felt like home

When the Wild Things Mend

Do you feel my tears
From so far away
Do you hear me whisper
Stay in my dreams

I wish you here
Every day
Every moment I hear
A song you sang
Every word you shaped
Still humming in the walls
Still warm against my skin

I wish you here
Every time
Something slips from my lips
And I remember
  This was yours first
Every time I find notes you left
And I trace the curves of letters
My fingers brushing the ghost of your being

I wish you here
But you're there
And there can't know
How blessed it is

*Not every ache
asks to be healed.*

20

What We Carry ما نحمله

يا نور عيوني
light of my eyes
they will not see the strength in your silence
or the prayers whispered under your breath
know that you are not the first
to walk into fire barefoot
or to close your eyes as they reshape your spine
or to smile while your bones are breaking

يا قطعة من قلبي
piece of my heart
know that you come from women
who whispered صبر جميل
and stitched patience into their skin
and wore forgiveness like perfume

صبرنا كان عبادة

and our hope
and our rebellion

they will call you soft
because they have not seen the steel
in a woman's longing
they will call you broken
because you bent to pray
instead of scream
let them talk and think they won

we build in silence
we rise in the dark

يا حبي الأول والأخير
my first and last love
you are not made of this world
you are threaded through it
like بسم الله whispered before a leap
like يا الله echoed after heartbreak
you are more than enough
even when the world pretends
you are too little
or you are too much

يا بنتي، يا عمري
my daughter, my life
in your hands you carry
the alphabet of our survival
A for ache
B for breath
C for carry on
D for دعاء whispered in the folds of night
and all the way to Z
for the zippers we've pulled over dreams
and reopened with faith

يا من علمتني معنى الأمومة
o you who taught me the meaning of motherhood
remember
your softness is not surrender
your tenderness is not a lack of strength
you do not need to be hard to be holy
you do not need to win to be worthy
you do not need to break to be acceptable

يا من تحلمين وأنا أحرس حلمك
o you who dream while I keep watch
one day
when you pass this truth
to your daughter
you'll do it in the language
we were never taught
but always knew

a language of women
of wounds that let the light in
then healed crooked
with scars that still shine

we are what we carry
and we carry everything
we carried it before you
and we carry it with you

until you are strong enough
to carry only what love should carry

نحن ما نحمله
ونحمل كل شيء
كلنا حملناه من قبلك
وسنحمله معك
حتى تصبحي قوية
لتحملي ما يحمله الحب فقط

21

The Essence of Us

جوهرنا
We stand on ground built by grit
The kind that doesn't fade with time
The kind that's carved into the earth
Like the marks on a blade
That's been sharpened on rocks
Through the years

On cave walls
Etched in ocher and ash
Are the outlines of women
Hips wide with wisdom
Hands raised in

دعاء
Prayer
Or
احتجاج
Protest

Proof that we were always here
نقشنا البقاء على الحجر
We carved our survival into stone
Always shaping, always surviving

نحن بنات الصبر
Daughters of endurance

For every challenge
There's a heart that beats strong
For every battle
There's a voice that sings
The song of our silent fight

We don't need medals to know our worth
We don't need titles to claim the crown we wear

Like horses in the wild
We're built for the chase
Not for the finish line, but for the race
In the moments of quiet, when the world is still
We are the light followed by thunder
Before the storm hits
The calm before the chaos

لا نخاف الصمت
We don't fear the silence
ولا نهرب من العاصفة
We don't run from the storm
We meet it with hands steady
With eyes that never blink

In the cup of coffee we drink
In the sweat of our brow

When the Wild Things Mend

In the hearts that still beat strong
In the blood that flows

بسم الله نمشي
We walk in the name of God
We are the ones who stand
The ones who fight
When the world turns its back

When the winds are wild
We hold our ground
When the sky cracks open
We don't flinch; we don't break
We stand
Like warriors of old
Like giants of now
Like souls that never yield

We are not measured by the gold we hold
Or the trophies on the shelf
We are measured by our deeds
By the hours we've spent in the struggle
By the lives we've touched
By the stories we've lived

نحن النار التي لا تنطفئ
We are the fire that doesn't burn out

والنور الذي لا يخفت
The light that never dims

والأثر الذي لا يمحى
The trace that cannot be erased

We are the essence
The ones who stay true
The ones who rise
مرة بعد مرة
Again and again

22

The Space Between

I asked for silence
not as a wall
but as a clearing
a breath in the thicket of noise
where I might find
my own pulse again

But you came with lanterns
shouting into the quiet
calling it abandonment
naming my retreat
a betrayal

You held out your ache
like a mirror
demanding I look
demanding I carry it
but I was already bent
beneath the weight of my own

I saw your grief
dressed in anger
your hurt masked as blame
You said "I'm devastated"
but it echoed like
"you did this to me"

On Hurt, Healing, and Heritage

I wanted to say
love does not cling
concern does not corner
hurt does not give license
to ignore the word no

Still, I answered with care
offered you warmth
even while my fingers burned
I said, "I hear you"
but you only heard
what confirmed your wound

In the end
there is a room
between us now
not locked
just quiet
A place where I can breathe
and you can decide
whether love can wait
without knocking

23

Inheritance

One knew the earth
like a story passed from womb to hand
not taught, just remembered

With calloused hands
and silence

Not the silence of absence
the silence that listens
   for rain
      for roots turning
         for life beneath the quiet dust

The other held pain
like a bowl too full
spilling grief into every corner
of the house

She didn't mean to bruise
with her distance
   but sorrow had shaped her spine
      and she forgot how to bend
         toward light

And then there was
the one under the shade of a tree
with questions instead of lullabies
books instead of embraces

Too many words
not enough warmth

She searched their eyes
  for a kind of knowing
    she never found
      only echoes
        of things unsaid

She wanted to be held
without being taught
and knew not what she was missing
except for emptiness
she could not name
wanted love
that didn't ache
before it arrived

She wished she knew
what the books spoke of
the images of mothers
loving and loved

Sometimes she would look at them
  in their quiet wars
    their stitched–up lives
      and wonder

When the Wild Things Mend

if she had been born
in the wrong story

They say blood remembers
but she remembered stars
and nights so wide
her body felt like a foreign object
on a planet
too loud
with need

So she called into the dark
like it was a mother too
like someone might answer
from the black velvet sky
"come home
you are not too much here"

Still
beneath it all
the soil waits

The pain folds
like cloth between generations
a bruised tenderness passes
hand to hand

And somewhere between
the dirt
the absence
the books
a wild seed
turns quietly
toward the sun

24

Safety Once Had a Scent

I did not ask for much
Not the return of her voice
or the warmth of her fingers
curled in mine

I only asked for the smell
of her
not even the whole scent
just a trace
left in the folds of an old scarf
or the pillow she once held
after turning her face away
from the weight of the world

I did not ask for time
to give her back
Time never gives
only softens the edges
until even the ache
starts to forget its reason

I asked for the memory
of her laugh
not the sound
but the way her shoulders
would rise
the way she'd tilt her head
like joy surprised her

But memory is cruel
It remembers pain with precision

and only lets the warmth
slip quietly through the cracks

I just wanted
to remember how she smelled
when she pressed me to her chest
How safety once had a scent
How I belonged
to someone without needing to earn it

Now
even her scent betrays me
The perfume bottle is empty
The shawl is washed
The air forgets
And I
I am left clawing at air
trying to hold love
by its shadow

They tell me to be grateful
to count the years I had her
But grief doesn't work that way
It counts what's missing

When the Wild Things Mend

in the softest places
in the scent that vanishes
the voice that won't echo
the name that fades
as I try to remember
what she called me
when no one was listening

I do not ask for miracles
I know the dead do not rise
I only ask
for the thing she wore
on the last day I saw her
creased with her scent
and folded, maybe
with the last touch
of her hands

Something that says,
"You are still loved"
even if she can't say it

I only ask
to be held
by something that once held her

And maybe then
just maybe
I'll stop calling into the silence
as if it remembers
better than I do

25

Beacons of Light

There are women
who move through the world
  like whispers of light
    dancing on water
      not always visible
        but always present

هن نور الهدى
They are nur al-huda
The light of guidance
Not loud
  just luminous
They don't always speak
  but their presence
    silences confusion

They are the unmarked compass
  in storms of uncertainty
  the hush before decisions
    the drop of eyelids for a wish
      the glow at the edge of a prayer

Those who burn quietly
سراج النور
Siraj al-nur
The steady lamps

They carry tenderness
  like a fire guarded in the wind

They warm the room
  without taking it over
They watch more than they speak
Their care is slow
  but it never forgets

They remind us
  strength need not be seen
    to be real

And when night stretches long
  some women become

ليال النور
Layal al-nur
Nights of light
They hold the stillness
  even as the world sleeps
They dream for those
  who have forgotten how

They are the du'a
  in the last third of the night

When the Wild Things Mend

the soft tear on a worn prayer mat
the quiet endurance
that keeps families whole

اللهمّ اجعل لنا من نورهن نصيبا
O Allah, grant us a portion of their light

There are women
who illuminate paths
just by surviving

ضياء الهدى
Diyaa al-huda
The radiance of guidance

Their pain
is not performance
Their strength
is not for applause

They walk with wounds
that teach others to heal
They fall
but they do not vanish
They grieve
but still they bless

And there are some
who will not dim
when asked to shrink

شمس النور
Shams al-nur
Suns of light
They blaze through injustice
   they soften no truth
Their heat is mercy
Their fire is revival
Their joy is not conditioned
   on permission

They are the women who say no
   so that others may say yes
      to what is right

None of this is a name
It is a way of being
A way of shouldering the world
   without letting it crush you

A way of folding grief
   into strength.
A way of making light
   in the places
      you were told to keep dark

And we remember
　those who have returned
　　to the One Who never forgets

اللهـم اغفر وارحـم
كل نفس
تحمل وجع الفقدان
لحبيب قد رحل

O Allah, forgive and have mercy
　on every soul
　　who carries the ache
　　　of a beloved now gone

ارزقهـم الصبر
واجعل فقدانهـم سببا للقرب

Grant them patience
　and make their loss
　　a reason for nearness to You

اجعل ذكراهـم نورا
ودعاءهـم رِفعة
وقلوبهـم مطمئنة بنورك
Make their remembrance a light

their prayers a rising
  their hearts at peace with Your light

So may we
  in all our forms
    all our wounds
      all our becoming
        be lit with something divine

Not perfect
  but luminous

*For your own
remembering.*

*Create space
here for what has
awoken in you.*

Afterword

Beautiful poems too good to stay hidden. Poems Sahar would share with us, often reluctantly, but ones I loved so much that I quietly began collecting them.

One year, for Sahar's birthday, we gathered them all, had them designed, and printed two copies at Officeworks—one for her, and one for myself. I called it Ajeeb (strange). Ajeeb because it was one of Sahar's favorite words, her go-to response to the oddities of the world. Maybe because the world is, in fact, strange.

That little gift planted a seed: Perhaps these poems could live beyond our private notes. Perhaps one day they could rest on shelves, waiting for others to find and connect with.

And that's how this book came to be. What began as quiet reflections has become something for the world to discover.

Yashar Kammoun

Every beginning seeps through endings
Every ending cracks us open
spilling light
into the aches we inherit

Through their whispers
we learn the shape of breath

About the Author

Sahar Dandan is a chemical engineer by training and a sustainability-driven executive by vocation. She holds a double degree in chemical engineering and science from the University of Sydney. Her passion for community development led her to shift careers, however, and she began creating programs for young refugees, Muslim women, and minority communities.

Alongside her professional and community work, Sahar continues to pursue studies in Islamic sciences and teach Islamic texts. She is currently the CEO of Greendale Garden Cemetery, where she leads efforts to integrate traditional burial practices with eco-conscious design.

Sahar began writing poetry at an early age, and this is her first published collection. This book is written at the gentle urging of her friends, who thought the world would enjoy her work as much as they do. She currently lives in Sydney, Australia, with her family and an ever-revolving menagerie of foster animals.

When the Wild Things Mend

We are a door with many rooms
holding our prayers
our rage
our laughter

> *our defiance*
> > *our brokenness*

> > > > *and we grow*
> > > > > *and we begin*
> > > > > > *again*

www.ingramcontent.com/pod-product-compliance
Lightning Source LLC
Chambersburg PA
CBHW021334060726
47591CB00006B/2013